Lemonade

Anouk Koch

LEMONADE

First Printing, 2024

Cover art by Carolyn Lord

A poetry collection

Anouk Koch

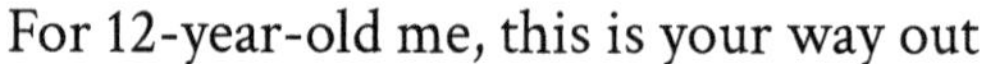

For 12-year-old me, this is your way out

This collection includes topics of abuse and violence, which may upset readers. Reader discretion is advised. //CW//

"She dealt her pretty words like blades."

- Emily Dickinson

Lemonade

Lemonade is just lemonade if you choose to ignore it

No need to look for the sour taste to graze your tongue
No need to look for it with all that is to come

There does not always have to be a sour taste
After the taste of
Sweet and simple fun
You choose to look for it
Because it is the only thing you have been taught to want

But if you look for it,
I believe sweetness can be found in the simplest aspects of this
Tiring, lemony life

Then again
Is it not easier to forget the sweetness and just remember
The taste of a past, lived life?

I say make lemonade into Fanta,
Into something sweet, bubbly to touch your tongue.
Lemonade can always be Fanta if you choose to see the bubbles

Scabs

Do not pick at scabs, they scar
Some wounds are meant to be sealed
Hurt hidden behind bandages

On some days when the sky feels heavier, hurt is better hidden,
Scabbed even if yet unhealed
They will scar
You are more than white lines crisscrossing skin

Do not pick at scabs, they leave marks of from the past

Consume

You leave red marks on my body
But
I want you to

I have grown used to seeing myself covered in them
I have not a spark of affection, with red marks on me
At least I have a wither of attention

Release it all on me as long as I can be assured your eyes still linger
My body yours to consume
Eat me whole if you please
A body no longer warm does not taste as good,
Taste while hot

You ate and marked every piece of my heart already
Do not hesitate now that I am but a carcass at your feet
Flesh feels comforting against your teeth
I hope once your mouth closes around a piece,
You will see all I have done to please
Even after death came to tease

Adult

I do not remember growing up,
A part of me has always been adult
The part that was left no choice

At seven standing in front of a court
The part that had to take care of herself
Because her parents were too busy shouting
The part that had to witness her brother slowly killing himself
The part that knew
She was never going to be good enough
No choice but to become grown-up
Always told how mature she was for her age

But God
Would I have loved to live in
The blissfulness of ignorance for just a little while longer
Before witnessing the cruelty
That life can bring

I wish
You could have held me
For just a little while longer before letting go
And oh, I know
You wish that too
Now I am already grown
Grown with the part that was bound to fail from the start

Intangible

I am myself intangible
For the world, for your touch and my own soul
Was I ever meant to be fully known,
If I cannot even figure out the reflection shown in the mirror?

Her smile estranges her further,
Her eyes seem distant longing for something unknown,
Her heart blows away in the breeze
She is to be nothing more than a puzzle piece

Another face covered by the world not accepting her fate,
A ghost meant to haunt herself more than anybody else

Picture Perfect

You never lay a hand on me on
Picture perfect days

I pray, may the day not turn to
Darkened desire

A red flame incensing your soul
Shows that you want me, my body reflected in the
Hazel harmony
Of your eyes scares me

An attraction that only arises if the day drags on too long
And your hands no longer in your control

Best I am kept your safe haven, your secret
Best I am nothing but your child
Of night

Try

I try, and I try, and I try
To pick up the pieces of the broken home you left behind
To prove to myself that I do not need your validation

I try, and I try, and I try
But I get cut
By the shards of glass still lying flat in this ruin,
That was once called a home
Can't you see all the blood that's flown since you've been gone?

I try to stop bleeding,
To prove to myself that I do not need your words
To soothe me at night in the darkest alleys of my mind

You were once my person
Now there is nothing of you within me to find
Just cuts on my fingers you left behind,
Cuts that sometimes when I'm alone at night still bleed,
Stains on the white bed sheets, you made me buy

Burn my Body

You look at me
And all I want to do is burn up my body

Let the ashes be the only thing that has felt your eyes gawking
Let my body be clean

Your eyes eat up all my dignity
I never allowed you to take the parts
That should have been mine from the start
I never said you had the right,
I could still feel your hands roam over me at night

I want to burn up my body
To leave you grasping the cold grey remains
Instead of my warm and oh-so-fragile autonomy

You call it your right,
Something that I am supposed to like
You shouldn't own my body
Your power will be nothing
If the only thing you can ruin is small particles of me
For I,
Will burn my body

Waves

The waves come crashing through,
Breaking on the rocks,
Making sure I do not get the chance to breathe in-between,

They pull me under with the impression of being my harbor
Yet the only thing I can is falter

Beneath the crashing weight of a home turned hostile
I lose the hope my heart had beat for

Remember

I remember the night a part of my soul left me
Oh, I remember it so vividly

I sat, sinking into the seat of your car
The world outside decorated with lights
Red, green and golden, flashing

I was twelve when I heard you screaming over the car radio
My feelings chewed out for me
By the voice that wouldn't let me breathe

I was the biggest horror
The worst mistake you could have made
On top of all, I didn't love you
Or so you said before your car drove off,
Away from the wet road until your screams turned silent,
I couldn't hear you
At all

Bleed onto the page

I want to create
Leave words on the page
But for once I wish I could write about
Falling in love
And not
Falling apart
I bleed with my words, they cut raw and deep
I bleed when I write so cascading
Restrained by the fear of losing all the blood within me

Hush

Hush, baby you can let go
Sleep child it is all right
Breathe deeply and do not be frightened
The night is a girl's best friend, it always has been

Hush, baby do not fight it
Sleep child and it shall be worth it
Let me sink my teeth into the flesh of your neck
You know you want it

Hush, baby do not lie
Sleep child and it shall be over in the morning light

Touch

You touched me,
The sun rose behind the mountain tops

Held me down,
The birds chirped at dawn

Words fell silent,
The leaves turned green then brown
Ending their journey back on the ground

Your demands tied me down,
I still woke,
My feet still carried me out of bed
You touched me, kissed me, held me

The world kept spinning anyway,
It never spun the same

Hold me

Hold me, please, even if your arms have grown tired over the years
Keep me close to your heart even if it wanders

Dry my tears even if yours could fill a river
Please I need to have what you never could

Cry me a river but do not expect me to understand,
I was in your clutches, your life was the main point of mine,

My tears turned into yours,
My sadness was overshadowed by the intensity of what you held,
My words were twisted
They cause you pain or so you say

Do not ponder any longer, I have learned
Do you need a hug? I know it has been hard for you in this world
I wish you could hug me
Only notice my arms in yours not the hurt of your own

Sinner

Father, for I have sinned

Cleanse me once the sun peaks behind the mountain tops
Until then I shall remain another creature of the night
Lured by sensations I should despise

What an excitement doing what you shan't brings!

What joy to not obey the rules you laid!

Perhaps I simply prefer being held by the dark
Remain a sinner in its arms

Desperation

What a sensation
To feel desperation to a stomach-churning degree
To breathe filtered since expansion might cause combustion
To have a weakened heart now strengthened
Exercise of beating for one that is still limp

My bones are breaking
While you leave aching footprints on my back

I crave deeply to be released from this strange infatuation
Going on like this might kill little old me

The blood in my veins has been restricted by your words
I need it released

Woods

I know these woods
I know their sounds
My lungs have breathed their air for years

Though there is a striking familiarity
I can still only crave to call it my home

These trees are haunted
Their leaves are dead
We killed them with whispers of dread
Your screams have brought them to tremble
I cannot walk past the indents you left in the crown of these trees
Everything here is haunted
You stained my woods

I long to forget the nights the grass harbored me from your grasp
There is no running from your past?

Saturn

You tell me I am worthless

Speak, as though you could not feel less
Look, with pure hatred

Yet my love seems everlasting
I cannot bring myself to stop the heartache
That takes form in your person

So, tell me I am worthless, feel nothing, hate everything
Still, I speak: "I love you to the moon and Saturn"

Caged

I had no way out,

Trapped in a cage fighting these walls, defeated by cold concrete
Trapped by a fist holding me in the tightest grip
Trapped by a piercing blue stare making sure I stay

Stripped from all power, left drowning in the depth of a ditch

Torn apart in the palm of your hand
Torn from real life
Torn away from my own heart

Release me

Or I shall release myself
Find my space in the frigid ground of this place
Never to be seen again
No reflection of my wounded face

What a pity to have to say, you are the reason I came

Honey

Her honeyed voice turned bitter
The admiration in her eyes seemed a fleeing bird
Flying too quickly,
I could not hold

And yes, I was told,
I would forever be her world
But that did not last long
As my limbs grew bigger and blue skies welcomed me better
Her eyes became cold, she did not want me anymore
A love meant to be unconditional
Ruptured by a mother not having any force in her feeble bones

Now I am but a withered leaf she chooses to walk on
All I needed was to be loved even by a broken soul's touch

Teeth

I am not the girl I set out to be,
Let me make grief a commodity

For both of us shall see the wounds, that cut of parts off me
You get a limb, and you get an eye
Feel the world I felt and see its pain; I made it
I am an object of entertainment,
Press a button to get the story of how I lost my childhood
Perhaps then we can share a laugh?

Cut out the pieces that please the hunger in you
Sharpen your teeth
Let them sink into me
I fall to my knees
Will you pray for me?

Slowly perish with no blood within me
Drained at their feet that is how they like to hold me
Vulnerability is all they need from me
The cost of a body at their feet

Muse

A muse in a white dress
It has yet not been stained
By the ignorance of her innocence

She glides over kitchen tiles
A ghost lost in the darkness of the night

She is yet to be harmed by the spitefulness she holds
A mirror to the sun's gaze, trying to show her beauty
Neither of them can truly acknowledge it,
They are blinded by the bright rays
Finding there, their own innocence

But blindness cannot be their state forever
Someday, they shall have to open their eyes, have them burn
Her dress shall now
Be stained in her own blood

Innocence is not an impermeable state

Tango

Only ever bright enough to see
One devil that played hell's tune, as I slept
One devil that supposedly ruined everything

But two partake in a twisted dance of tango,
Don't they?

He takes one step
Then you do
One step of hatred and a second of guilt

Back and forth gliding over the dance floor as I watch
Do not hide anymore, for I know
Tango cannot be danced alone

So long as you love me

Ergo dum me diligis
Prepared to bring you the sun if you shall desire it
Willing to burn down the world
Leaving only the taste of ash

Ready for any task you dare throw at me,
It does not seem as hard knowing you love me

I tried bleeding myself dry,
It was never enough to earn an ounce of your love

I try now with all that I have
To give your desires a path
Ergo dum me diligis, my love

Mother

Tell me how to be
So you can love me enough
I want to give you what you need,
So your arms do not get estranged from my touch
I will bring the world to your feet, if you please,
The world might be able to weigh you down
You cannot flee anymore
Mother tell me,
What do you need?

Body and soul

I could not watch you walk away
The memory blurred by tears
I could not watch you leave
Our world crumbled to pieces at my feet

A fallen castle
A bucket full of tears
Is that all you left behind?

I am not a soul, not a body
Only ruins of emotions and pieces of empty cloth

Cloth stained
Life shattered
Time fleeing into the past
I am not a soul, not a body now that you left me behind

Monster

He took all that she had
Away from her dying arms

She gave everything,
And he gladly ate her heart
With bloodstained lips, he smiled

We know, he ruined her
He could not help his grin,
Blood on his teeth
Seeping with pride

A monster, a monster, a monster

Gnawing the flesh of dead, still breaking bones
Only to be satisfied

We let him!

Sleep

Shh, night has come, it demands silence
Shh, let your heavy head rest on soft pillows
Shh, let sleep take you to wonderland

It is no help resisting
The moon has strength, and it forces you to sleep

Shh,
Let your mother's arms close around what used to be your body
Once its call has come you have no right not to answer

Hush, it is softer than it seems
Parting might appear hard, but fighting is surely harder

Relax your arms and let it carry you
Hush, baby, it is simply life falling asleep

Acknowledgments

Thank you to all the people that kept on insisting I do this, never letting me give up on writing and believing fully that this publication would happen. Even if I was a very intent seven-year-old whose storytelling voice was certainly not found in poetry and rather in stories of fierce vampire dogs. You believed anyway.

Thank you, mom, for insisting on countless visits to art galleries and any cultural or literary event you could find, no matter where in the world we were. You made me into this. Thank you also to my dear ones who read, reviewed and put up with my poetry: Anne Gambling, Lionel Carnot, Melisa Güzelgün, Agostin Koch, Leon Koch, Sarah Koch and Mira Zeier.

And thank you to everyone who stood by my side during the whole the process.

Printed in the USA
CPSIA information can be obtained
at www.ICGtesting.com
CBHW061636221124
17856CB00014B/655